The Chosen One

Terry Delane Kidd Jr.

Dedication

To those who inspired me, thank you. Without your support, I would not be here today. In addition, thank you God for the gift of life.

Forward

This book has taken me over a decade to complete. Consequently up till now only a hand full of people have read even a single poem from this work. I contemplated many times whether to publish it or not, and so here it is.

This book is over a controversial topic, the "end times". It is about a man and his journey through the end times as he discovers his destiny. It also includes personal thoughts during his trials and tribulations.

I have an interesting background in the Christian faith. My mother's father and one of his brothers are retired ministers. In addition, one of my mother's brothers is a minister now. All preached in a Pentecostal church; the denomination is Church of God. I have seen many things through my life that I will never be able to explain. Nevertheless, I have faith that they did happen.

To understand the story fully, it is best to read it front to back. I challenge all who read this book to keep an open mind and an open spirit while reading it.

Table Of Contents

Part I Prophesy Untold: **Epic of the Chosen One**

The Unknown Object

Act I

There it sat, still motionless, not a sound,

Nothing, only silence-

I looked at it from a distance

Trying hard to make out what it was

From where I was, afraid to move closer

To the unknown object;

Then I moved closer, still trying to get a glimpse

Of what the object was

But still afraid for what might happen;

Closer, closer I got, still wondering,

Still afraid, unsure of what might happen

If I saw what it was; as I got closer I could see

A better picture of the object;

It was kind of like a person sitting in a chair

While I was looking, I heard my name called out

I looked around but did not see anybody or anything-

I walked on, still wondering,

Still trying to figure out what it was

That I saw in front of me;

Then I could see that it was a person

I gave it a name, Mr. Unknown

I walked on; closer and closer-

Wanting to know who this Mr. Unknown is;

Then, just that moment, he vanished without a trace

But wait there he is over there-

I ran as fast as I could trying to catch up to him

Wanting to know who he really was;

Faster and faster I ran-

It seemed like I would never get close enough to grab him;

Then, it seemed I was getting closer

Gaining a foot every second-

I did not have time to look where I was going

Or even to look at my surroundings;

I just ran as hard as I could

Twenty, ten, five feet,

I reached out my arm,

Grabbed his shoulder with my hand,

And turned him around; I saw his face-

Mr. Unknown was me

Act II

I looked into his eyes and he looked into mine

Without a flinch he turned around,

Clapped his hands, and vanished

But this time with me;

All of the sudden, there was light

We were in a church

As I looked around, I saw people-

Some I knew, others I have never seen before

It was a wedding but whose I asked-

He didn't say a word;

He only took me to the back of the church

I could not see much

Just the backs of everyone's heads;

I looked at the groom

And the bride to see who they where

As they were turning to kiss,

I noticed the groom was me;

I looked at Mr. Unknown and we vanished

Before I got to see who the bride was, my bride-

While in darkness, I asked him who she was,

Why he had shown me this,

And where he was taking me next;

We then appeared at a house

I asked whose it was

But he would just stand there and not say a word

I heard footsteps and then I saw myself again

I was getting a coat out of the closet-

Then I heard more footsteps coming from the stairs;

That is when I saw her-

She turned around; I saw her face;

My bride was Melissa-

I looked at Mr. Unknown and then back at myself

Melissa said thanks for coming over;

It feels good to get it out in the open finally

I saw myself leave-

I looked at Mr. Unknown

And we vanished again;

We ended up at the same place we had started from

He stared into my eyes;

Then for the first time he spoke

He said, "Now I leave you with the past behind you

And your destiny awaiting and undecided"

In that moment I wake up in bed,

The first day of the rest of my life-

For I have to get ready for college and adulthood

I will be going into unmarked areas of the world

As for Mr. Unknown, I never had the dream again;

But until this time I have always believed

That it was God that I saw in my dream

Act III

I am back, someone said in the far of distance;

I heard something walking closer to me,

He appeared; Mr. Unknown was back-

As he walked up to me,

I noticed things felt and looked different;

I thought he had left me,

That he would never return;

The question was why he did-

I looked straight into his eyes and I saw wisdom;

Not just any wisdom but the wisdom of the past,

The present, and the future;

Then he spoke saying,

"I have come back to tell you of a story

About a man and his Great Journey

To find knowledge, wisdom, and truth;

This man once he finds these three things,

Will then have everlasting knowledge

Of both the world and the things not of this world;

He will find wisdom to guide his knowledge

Through the right path;

He will have truth of both himself

And of the one thing he has sought out

Through the journey:

The truth of the beginning of life and beyond;"

I looked at Mr. Unknown and asked him,

Who this man was-

He looked at me

And said, "There is more to the story;"

So I listened to him-

He went on saying,

"This man will find it difficult
On this journey, he will have
Happiness and pain, victory and defeat,
Love and hate, and peace and war;
This man will have riches
Beyond what he has ever seen
And he will be tested,
If he passes, he will keep what he has gained
If he fails, he will lose everything
And become poor as he was before"
I looked into is eyes and asked,
"Who this man was he was talking about"
He only replied, "There is still more to tell"-
So I listened trying to be patient
He said, "This man and his Great Journey,
Once it is completed, will become a legend
And will pass through the ages
Until the end of time;"
He stopped and looked at me
And said, "now your question"
I asked him a final time
"Who is the man you speak of?"
Mr. Unknown looked at me puzzled
As he stared into my eyes for a moment-
He spoke saying, "you" and then vanished
Act IV

I stood in awe and confused

When I realized what he had said;

I realized my future was in my hands-

All that I have ever known or thought

Was thrown out the window-

All I ever dreamed possible

Would never happen-

For I knew that this Great Journey

Would be something so tremendous

That I could never do it alone;

And I knew then that Mr. Unknown was God,

That my life had just begun-

Not how I would have seen it,

But what God had planned for me;

So now, the journey begins

I Fear

I have been in the valley

I have seen the hurt, the pain

I have felt the sorrow of my heart

And I have heard the cries of my soul

I have been in the bottom, very deepest of holes

With no light, no sound, and no hope,

I have had the thoughts of loneliness

I have felt the toils of time

I have cried out in the silence of a large, loud crowd

But no one heard me on this land-

I have seen the top of the mountain

I have seen the people pass me by

I have tried and tried to escape this place

With no luck on my human strength

I fail to find my way up and out;

Then I remember the word of God,

The promise he made

Found in myself stairs to above,

Climbed them, to the top up high

Out of the valley, that deep, dark valley

And into that great bright light-

Now on the top of that great mountain I can see

The next valley that lies ahead

And even with my new hope inside,

The promise, and the faith,

I fear, I fear, I fear-

In and out the next valley I go, is this the end?

I don't know; I get to the top and I find

Another valley that is mine

In and out, I find myself

Caught in a limbo of love and hate

I know I can make it through and get to the light

Reaching to the top once again,

Yet I fear, I fear, I fear-

I have seen the hurt around the world

I have felt the pain and the torment,

And the effect on peoples lives

I have seen the horror, the death, the lame,

And the children;

I cannot get their voices out, out of my mind,

Out of my head,

Never-ending, never any silence-

But I remember what Jesus said

And with a single prayer of faith, I can rest again,

And yet I fear, I fear, I fear-

I have seen hell with my eyes

I have seen the conversion, the contrast,

And the place I hate

I have seen the darkness within the flame,

Within the fire, within the light-

The coldness of hell, so frightening,

The wails of the people burning

Tormented forever and ever;

I have felt the soars, their faces so scared

A place of cries made out to the one they cast out,

Turned away from for the world,

From the one who could have saved them,

From the one called Jesus;

Forever locked in a place of horror,

Of an odor of burnt flesh and moans,

And I fear, I fear, I fear-

I have seen the gateway from that world to the next

Through the light and to heaven

I have seen the green meadows, the orchard of trees,

The running brooks, and the calm lakes;

I have seen that Golden City

With gates of pearl, streets of gold,

The angels, the elders, and the people-

People who made it through the toils,

Who made it to see the Lord our God

I have seen the throne and the one who sits upon it

I have heard the praises

And still I fear, I fear, I fear-

I have seen the red dragon,

The one who comes for the virgin lady

To take the baby from her womb,

I have seen the angels all lined up

Ready for what awaits;

I have seen the spilt blood in God's name

I have seen the Anti-Christ rise on earth,

Taking control, ruling, knowing time is short-

I have seen the tribulation and the pain in it

The suffering of borderline Christians left behind,

I have felt their sorrow, and their pain;

Hatred toward God and their souls decay

But the few who make it get ready to die,

To die for their Lord,

Who will take them home and beyond the sky

And I fear, I fear, I fear-

I have seen the destruction wrought by him,

The one who started it long ago-

Who thought he was the one supreme;

I have seen Armageddon, the battle of end,

The blood already rising up from the ones there-

Filling the land, forming a lake, the death,

And yet, the hope of a better day;

I have seen the end, the victory

I have seen God's children win

I have seen the devil, that slippery snake,

Thrown into Hell, forever locked away

I have seen the New Jerusalem coming down

I have seen the New Kingdom arise on Earth

I have seen the peace, the love,

The wonderful life it will be

And yet, I fear, I fear, I fear-

I have seen it all, felt it, heard it,

I know the end, the way it will be

I have seen God's entire plan

And still, I fear, I fear, I fear-

I know how to gain all that is mine

I know how to see my Lord

I know his word, his way

Yet though I am far away

He will always be with me

Carrying me through the rough waters,

Helping me to see it through

Yet I fear, I fear, I fear-

The end is closing, fast approaching

So much to do, so little time

I have not yet given all to him

My Savior, my Lord, my Creator-

I have not yet shunned the world

And I fear, I fear, I fear-

I fear I have no time; I fear the end is now;

I fear I have lost my last chance to see God now,

To be in heaven, to sing God's praises,

To walk with angels, to walk along the brooks,

The orchard of trees, the green meadows,

And the golden streets-

Though I fear I do all I can to make my life right,

To claim what was mine, and to gain what was lost

My faith, my love, my hope, my wisdom, my soul,

I do what I can to stay just,

So as Judgment comes

I can see my heavenly home and be with Jesus,

The angels and my God

To live forever and ever with my new family

To know all, see all, and believe in hope once again

And yet I know all this is to be,

To come, and for me to see

I fear, I fear, I fear-

I fear not what death brings to all,

But what life offers me another day

Identity Lost

As I think back to years past

I see myself as someone I do not know

For all through life I have been

What others had made me to be

I thought to myself, how could I conform-

My identity all a blur, my life but an image

An image of what others expect me to be

For I have wasted years on something

That is not mine-

What can I do; what can I say;

How will I stop this roller coaster ride

Of my demise from peoples eyes-

Those same eyes that made me,

Criticized and scorned me for what I have become

For God only knows how I have tried,

Tried to change, make myself the way I chose to be

And be what God requires of me

Though I have tried, these people,

My so-called friends

Still see me as what I have always been

But when will the madness stop

And allow me to be what I have lost,

What I have never seen, myself, my own identity,

Day in and day out, every time I try to change

I fall back farther to my past,

The past that haunts me, reminding me of my life,

The only life I have known-

For once, I wish I could get ahead

Find my true self and climb out of my past,

As I wonder what my life could have been

If I had only been my true self

What wonderful things and places I could have seen

The people I could have met

And yet, though I wonder and think,

What if I did become that person-

I would have never met the people I knew now,

Never to have shared my life with them

A new person I would have become

Just as I am now, I would not know myself then-

I know all I have to care about

Is what I think of myself

And do what God requires me to do-

Never worrying about what others might say

Or what others might do

I am who I am, I always say

But when you do not know who you are

It is hard to say that phrase,

And yet, through it all,

From wondering what could have been

And from the little I know now

I see this constant, the one identity that counts

I am God's child

Secret Life

Looking but never seeing,

Hearing but never listening,

Hopes and dreams of a thoughtless world

Become lost in the dark-

Intentions of good but always a bad outcome

From those of the world;

Apart from the whole, the truth-

As a man sees and listens to a world of destruction,

Apart from it; yet, apart of it;

Trapped between, in a void that does not exist

Waiting for the end, anticipating,

Knowing the outcome,

Yet never to know his part, his will, his truth;

Knowing he will not see it

Till he confesses of his darkness-

The one he sees not,

Because his heart sees not himself

Always tormented to see the darkness,

Hell, Satan, Armageddon,

Everyone's place in the whole, the truth

But never his own;

Always shown what he could and might even miss

Heaven, Jesus, his God,

The God who made him from his own breath-

This man becomes no man,

More than human but less simultaneously;

He becomes the one to see it all through

To the end, to see all there is and will be;

He becomes the watcher,

A man born never to die by man's hands

But only by the hand of God-

Destined to be the keeper of night;

He will be like the space of time

Between sunrise and sunset-

A void of nothing, only himself,

His very existence, exists not-

Only one act can save him

But he wishes not to be saved

For he has been fooled, cheated;

Been made a lie by his own blindness

He goes on in procrastination, fixed to his path

But keeping a portion of his faith,

A faith so perplexed and weak-

He gave in to his maker

Not once, not twice but three times;

All failed, all gone a waste;

No more will he see God's hand of mercy

He tries but sees it not

And he knows the end draws near-

And his first journey ends

But not the Great Journey;

The tribulation awaits him,

The place of his demise and of his resurrection-

To take his place as keeper of the night;

He shall no longer go by is birth name

But be known as the watcher;

Like a thief in the night, he will build his army-

Those that are of him,

People caught in their own void

And of the whole void-

Taking their place by his side

Till the end, till Armageddon

Between The Fork

As I traveled down the road,

Down the road I knew so well;

I saw my life flash around me

Like a big picture show or movie;

As I watched and looked about,

I could see the good and bad times,

The happy and sad times,

The ups and downs

Of my struggling walk with Christ;

As I walked on and thought,

I came across a fork in the path;

The old turning point of life

Where many have come to but few sought out-

I stood to choose which way to go

And noticed someone behind me;

I just watched as the person chose a path

As I kept watching people go by

Choosing their path, the way for them,

I noticed that only a few went down a certain path-

The path that was so straight and narrow;

I wondered why this was so;

I realized that the world had more to offer

But in all reality which is better, quantity or quality;

As I thought and thought,

I went back to what I had learned,

What I had seen and heard-

I realized at that point what I needed to do;

I sat down on the corner of the two,

Right in the middle of the two paths-

I tried to tell people about what I learned

What I knew to be the better choice;

As I did this, I found it difficult

To get through to some;

They wanted the world,

And all the while they asked,

"Are you going to chose?"

I quickly found out you lead by example,

So I started down the less used path

But I quickly wanted to go back

Just to tell one more to cross over;

I realized that it was drawing me back,

Back to the world, so I turned around-

I did this several times, back and forth

Wanting so much to tell

But all the while needing to press forward;

As I stood at a safe distance down the path,

Just far enough out from the pulling sensation

But close enough to yell,

I tried to get people to follow,

And more and more they chose the other path;

I became discouraged and sad-

Realizing if I stood still I would fail;

And if I moved on, I would lose those I love;

And if I go back, I will lose my soul;

I had to make my choice, my stand-

Either I am for Christ or not;

I pondered and after a moment, I fell in tears-

How could I leave the others behind?

So, I made a sign of what truly lies before me;

I ran as fast as I could to the fork

And I pushed the sign in the ground-

I looked one last time and walked down the path;

The road was hard but I persevered through-

It went on for miles and miles

But I knew that no matter what

The end of this road was eternal life with God,

And that all the trials and tribulations,

The hurt, the sorrows, and the pains,

And the scorns and the cruelty of others

Will pass away and the tears will melt away

By happiness and joy and laughter-

Because God is all I want and desire,

And to those I leave behind I pray

That you will see the sign at the fork

And follow the road home

Struggles' End, Souls' Last Stand

My soul crashes

Through the waves of sorrow and pain-

Entering constantly into a convoluted world

In search of a place of solitude-

Longing for the day it will again live free

From the torment, from the complacency-

Breaking down the strong hold of chains

That holds me back from heaven;

My soul fights to step up to the path-

The trials and tribulations are many and hard;

Looking for a hard place, a rock to step on-

Finding none, my soul pushes on down the path,

Stepping through the ups and downs,

Hoping to find that rock to rest my broken soul;

My soul presses through the demons

That laugh in my face-

Seeing the ones I love used as pawns

By the one, Satan, to drag me further down-

Keeping me further from the rock on the path,

I realize more than ever that I must fight;

My soul denies its struggle

Between right and wrong, good and evil-

Leaping out on a tattered and torn faith

That sees nothing, feels nothing,

But knows he's there, surrounding me,

Fighting the demons for me,

Knowing my way has been hard

And the rock is within reach

But still so far that my eyes cannot see;

My soul inches farther and farther along-

One-step forward, a million steps back,

That rock, the foundation I need to rest upon

Lies so far away, yet so close-

I can feel its smooth surface on my fingers;

More and more I urge myself to move on;

Fight the demons; fight the waves of despair,

To reach the rock, the foundation,

The way out of the valley my path has taken me;

The steep mountain that lies ahead-

The tip reaches the heavens, how can I go on;

My soul cries out in anguish and defeat

For it knows I have been beaten down;

Praying for a way out, I see a rock up ahead

Protruding out of the foot of the mountain-

Thinking if I could only make it to the rock

Then I could rest my battered and broken soul;

I press and push, struggle with each step-

The side of the rock is within reach;

I can almost feel the tip of the rock

Only to be stricken with a stuck foot,

Then the other and just out of reach

I fall down and weep;

My soul sees the comfort of the rock,

Urges me to fight, to reach our goal-

My body cannot endure anymore;

Battered, beaten, tattered, torn,

The pain becomes unbearable-

The hurting feelings of sorrow and demise;

Reminding me of the promise,

And I reach out to grab the rock to pull myself loose,

To tear down the stronghold of Satan's grip;

The struggle was intense-

Every moment was harder and harder;

Then, just in a blink of an eye,

I reached the corner of the rock-

Pulled myself out and up upon the rock;

Exhausted, I sit; my broken down soul rests

Knowing the rest of the way will be rougher;

My soul looks up from its frail state

And whispers, "All is not lost,

For the next rock lies ahead;

Gain your strength for the next leg of your climb

For with each passing rock draws you closer

To the mountain top where heaven lies,"

So I look up, and I do see the next rock for me;

And though I know it will be tough,

With the trials and tribulations,

The torment, the anguish and pain,

The suffering and despair,

I know I will make it for there is help along the way-

A rock, a foundation, a place to rest my soul;

And when I reach the top of that steep mountain,

My soul will be free in its new home

The Chosen One

Long before a master plan,

Before God thought of man and of angels,

Eons of life in dark emptiness, he lived alone-

Contemplating on whether to create a perfect place,

Long before he built his kingdom in heaven,

And the thought of his son, Jesus,

Who was the perfect gift to humanity,

Who gave his life for you and I,

Long before Lucifer's revolt in heaven,

Before God cast him and his followers out

Condemning them to eternal death,

God had one in mind, the Chosen One;

This man would come from the depths of sin,

From his chains of bondage in his mid-life years

To learn, to develop, to rise into a leader,

To lead those left in the Great Tribulation

Who searched out God in those years of despair,

Lost without the grace of God,

Doomed, if not reached, to rot in Hell;

In those years before the end,

He would become aware,

And yet, condemn the truth-

Make it a lie made by Lucifer;

A constant battle within himself over his future,

A future as of a black canvas as he would say-

Slowly he becomes aware

Of God's master plan for him-

Every waking moment of his life prepares him

Not only for his life now

But for the Great Tribulation;

Little does he realize

The purpose of his tattered faith,

The failing grace he lives in-

Preparing him for those graceless years from God;

The Chosen One will leave all he had ever known,

And face the enemy from every way, everywhere-

Fighting man and demon alike till the bitter end,

Unafraid of death, unafraid of the loss,

Knowing his eternal life hangs in the balance-

But he is not without faith or the Holy Spirit

For in those years before the beginning of end,

His soul cries out for one last touch-

Receiving such a power, an awakening-

Blessed with everything he ever wanted,

The feeling of peace and happiness,

Not only from God, but from one special girl

Who lightened up his life

With one last touch of love,

Only to lose it for the greater good of all;

His sacrifices only out-weighed by God and Jesus-

Fighting along side

With the prophets of the Tribulation,

Reaching out to a sick and perverse world,

Building an army of soldiers for God

To battle the false prophet,

The Anti-Christ, and Lucifer;

The Chosen One will see many things,

Ungodly creatures tormenting humans,

Sickness, disease, loss of death, the cries for death,

The destruction of cities, towns, countries, cultures,

Brother against brother, sister against sister,

Families fighting themselves,

And the desecration of God;

In those Tribulation years,

People will forget and surrender-

He will lose many to Lucifer and his armies;

Many will take the mark to survive

Not knowing they are giving up

Their only chance of life; those who fight,

Will see their families murdered to break them-

Those who last will be killed, made martyrs of God;

But the few remaining will stand beside him,

Fighting evil, a battle of battles, a constant struggle

Of empty victories and hard pressed defeats;

Through the Great Tribulation, they will see

Their very soul's intent and the fears

That haunt them at night;

The Chosen One will find himself

Beaten down along the way,

Struggling not to give in as he did in the last days-

He will cry out in despair

To God asking to release him-

And then, realizing his place, he will rush in,

Fight harder and harder with every battle,

Not sleeping for days until done with the job-

Waiting until the final day comes, the end of the war,

When Jesus will return

To throw Lucifer in Hell,

Locked for a thousand years

While peace reins on Earth;

And the Chosen One can finally rest

Knowing it is finished,

The end of the years of struggles and battles-

His tattered and torn graceless faith is renewed

As he receives his crown and places it at God's feet;

He kneels down and cries holy, holy, holy,

Holy is the Lord God Almighty,

Who was, is, and is to come;

And as he looks up

And sees the faces surrounding him,

He cries, for those souls he fought for

Now live in Heaven-

Those same people he gave his life to save,

The strangers that in the last days he never knew

As he prepared for the war he could not imagine;

As the Chosen One stood from his knees,

God spoke and all listened-

He said with a thundering voice, "I am well pleased,

Enter into my kingdom and suffer no more,"

And as I watched I remembered,

That there were not supposed to be tears in heaven;

But as I watched the Chosen One enter Heaven,

I saw a tear fall from his eye-

He turned and looked at me as he spoke

He said, "Remember what you have seen

For your time is at hand,"

And then I knew who I had seen was me

Bedtime Thoughts, Bedtime Fears

In the darkness of the night,

I find my solitude

From those things that haunt me-

I glare into the shadows

Of a once known self;

Seeing the fears that torment my life,

The fears of guilt and death-

Not the death of flesh,

But of a spiritual death

That walks the Earth searching,

Longing for freedom from captivity;

I find myself not afraid

Of those things present in my eye,

But of those unknown, unseen

By my soul's sleepless sight

Looking to the heavens for comfort;

Finding only a silenced ear,

I tremble in fear of life-

For another day brings temptation

That can send me to Hell,

And all I can do is pray

That in my darkest hour

He will come to rescue me

From the coldness, the loneliness,

The complexity of my walk;

My future, ever so distant,

Ever so blurred from my sight-

Destined in obscurity

From me till my very last breath;

And as I lay in bed

Expecting at any moment

For a demon to attack,

To laugh, tormenting me

With the thought of my death,

I ask God to watch over me

In hopes that by the single utter

Of Jesus' name, I could feel safe;

The windows knock and shake,

The creeps and bumps,

The noise outside my window

Ever so start- ever so become more evident,

And I tremble, as my eyes want to shut;

Tired from the battles during the day,

Worn from the fighting with demons-

Knowing that if I sleep I could die,

And if I do not sleep,

Those I am here to save will suffer

Because I am not rested to fight another day;

So I speak, uttering a language not my own,

And the peace falls in the room-

Outside, the silence begins again,

And I know He has come-

The fight will begin tomorrow,

The battle will rage on

Until the end, until the peace can stay;

And my journey is over

As Jesus returns for his lost soldiers,

And I look up and see my home

Revelations Revealed: **Ground Zero,** The Final Days

I have seen this day come

I have seen what lies ahead

I have seen God's children called up

I have seen the demons, Satan

I have seen the world become Hell;

For all these millennia after

Jesus' birth has lead to

What is about to take place;

The world has lost her way

The people have lost sight of God,

Of his word, of his grace;

For Grace will soon leave

And damnation of our Earth

Will take its place-

The time will come

When all will be lost and

All will be gained; for those few

In these last days that see

With their spiritual eye

What lays ahead, their lives will soon change,

And the beginning of the end,

The end of all humanity's way,

Replaced with suffering

And deathless pain;

For the one, Satan, will soon rise

His army of demons, of lost souls

Who will be left in the tribulation

To torment, to destroy, to battle

Those who will defy them;

Who will fight the good fight

Against that which seeks them out

Like animals; I can see the signs,

And I know the time is near;

A new Babylon, a new tower of Babel-

The world coming closer together

With technology racing out of control;

Rumors of war, talks of peace,

In the place so held dear by God,

Israel is a nation once again

As prophecy has foretold,

And Palestine is again rising up

To take Canaan once again;

But there will come a time

When Palestine will fall,

And when she does, Satan

And his forces will be soon upon us;

I have been watching, waiting

For those I know to be of God

To be saved, on their way to heaven,

To be called up; I know when

THE CHOSEN ONE

All of God's children have left

In the rapture, my time has come

To go out, call my army,

And reach out to those left behind,

To spread the gospel, to wait

For the prophets to arrive

So that they might give me guidance

In those terrible days;

I can see the major players

In these last days-

China with her unlimited force of soldiers,

Russia and her former states

With such a nuclear force

That it could wipe out the world,

North Korea, Iraq, Egypt, Lebanon,

And so many others around

God's chosen people since the dawn of man;

I can see the Anti-Christ, the false prophet

Rising even today, the powers

Of Europe, such a great common wealth,

Such a history of war and disease;

I can see Great Britain

Who was once our enemy

And our friend, leave the United States

Alone for the kill;

Though most of the fighting is in Europe

And Asia, the United States

Will be a broken nation,

For she has fallen from God's grace,

She has left her foundation, her calling

To put the world right again;

She will lose her commander in chief

In the rapture and be left without a leader-

All Hell will break loose

As the end will be here

And I will begin my path;

And dawn and evening has broke;

I will sleep for one more night-

A good rest, a long rest;

And in my dreams I see the future-

Every day the thoughts I have done

Something before have become

Stronger, and I know the end is near;

And in my dreams that night

I saw those I love gone,

And the end had come,

And Jesus had taken home God's children;

I woke up the next morning

Feeling like something was different,

The house was empty,

And all were gone about their business

So I went to work, and as I was driving,

THE CHOSEN ONE

I saw in front of me cars

On the side of the road

Empty but with clothes,

And I knew the end had come;

I stopped and got out of the car

And looked up to the sky,

And in me I hear a voice calling,

Saying, "It has begun"

Psalms 151: A Psalm of the Chosen One, The Final Battle with Satan

Safe in the brightness of day,

My enemies cannot reach me-

For the light of my Lord and Savior

Empowers me, drives me,

Strengthens me as I prepare to enter

Into the enemies stronghold-

Praises to He who walks with me,

Talks with me in the light of day;

It is almost the third hour,

And the battle is at hand;

I must prepare; I must pray

To my Savior, Jesus Christ

And ask for the spirit, who flows

Like the wind from east to west

To protect me as I enter

Into the enemies stronghold;

Praises to He who fills me with His love,

With His spirit, with His strength;

Hear me O' Lord; hear my prayer-

For You are worth of my praise;

You lift me up; You help me

Walk across the waters of the sea-

Send Your Holy Spirit down to me,

Empower me with Your strength

So that I might defeat my enemies;

Glory to God in the highest

For You are worthy to be praised;

I lift Your name to the heavens-

Praises to He who comforts me

In the night as my enemies surround me;

The sixth hour approaches

And night is coming;

My enemies will be on their way

To fight me, to over power me,

To pull me down into the pits of Hell-

I light the lamp; reserve the oil;

As I wait for the angels to appear,

To fight the demons that empower

My enemies, Satan himself comes tonight

To conquer me, for I am the last

Stronghold on Earth; I am the last one

Who stands for Jesus in the final days

Of the great tribulation, in the

Final battle before Jesus' return

And takes the throne;

Praises to He who I adore

With all my heart, all my body, all my soul;

Night has come; the enemies are here-

My soldiers stand ready to fight

Till the end, till their deaths

For a greater cause, a greater good,

The end of the Anti-Christ's reign on Earth;

For though this battle is about to start,

The war has been upon us for almost seven years,

And tonight is the final stand for God;

O' Lord my God whom I call out to,

Send Your angels down to me,

To hold the demons back

So that I might fight their legions

Of human soldiers who come for me,

To defeat me, and murder the last

Of Your faithful in this great tribulation;

O' father in Heaven I seek Your face;

I seek Your voice; I seek Your presence,

And though I know You are far,

Far from this place, You are in my heart

And my soul; praises to You

O' mighty God in Heaven

For the time is at hand, and Your

Faithful servant will soon enter

Into the enemies camp;

I seek a sign that You have not

Forgotten us in our time of need;

Praises to He who sits upon the throne;

Praises to He who shall set

His throne on Earth;

The battle is here, my enemies

Are upon me, surrounding me-

The struggle is overwhelming,

But in the darkness of the night

I find strength in God's word,

And my faith in Him empowers me

To press forward; all through the night

I fight principalities; I fight Satan;

I fight that which is evil and despised

In God's eyes; for though the

Demons come for their freedom,

I have nothing to fear

For I have a savior who died for me,

Setting me free over two millennia ago;

And if I should die in the battle,

The war is already decided,

And God's people have already won;

Praises to He who set us free

From all sin, all oppression,

All that death was;

Praises to He who comes at dawn

To lead us to Heaven,

And to send the demons and Satan

To Hell, and bring a new dawn

For His people;

And so it was at the ninth hour

That God sent His only

Begotten son to us,

And all the warrior angels followed-

A loud trumpet and voice called

High above the clouds,

And with three words

Spoken from His spirit saying,

"It is done,"- the ground shook

And opened up under the demons

And swallowed them up;

Satan stood as Jesus descended,

Saying, "your day is through";

And so it was so that Satan

Was cast down to Hell;

Praises to He who can do all and more;

Praises to He who brings the new dawn

Neo- Genesis: **The new dawn of humanity**

The thousand-year reign has ended,

God has done away with the old-

He has put away heaven and earth;

Where, it doesn't matter

For he is now creating a new beginning,

A new heaven and earth;

Satan is no more, for God

Has cast him into the outer darkness-

His demons, long ago angels of God who fell

Are with Satan, forever bound in

Eternal darkness; Hell is no more

In the center of our world-

God has moved it without missing a spot;

The lost souls forever burning along side

With Satan, the demons;

God's children are now whole,

No longer bound by human flesh

Or human mind; we have been transformed

Into a new creature, into a new race;

Humanity is no more, for we are spiritual beings,

Boundless in our travels-

We can move across the universe

Without the aid of technology,

Without the aid of a spacecraft;

The universes are our new back yard-

We will become guardians

Of all living creatures, plants, races;

So much to explore, so much to see-

An endless journey to travel;

We shall live for eternity and beyond,

We will see things that our former human mind

Could have never comprehended;

I have seen so much in my time-

For I have been human, and I am now made new;

I went through the last days,

I fought in the tribulation,

I lived through the millennia reign of Jesus,

And now I have realized

That all those things I saw cannot compare to what

I will soon witness, and will soon see;

For I am now immortal; my humanity cast away

With the Old World, the old ways-

For now, I get to help in building

A new earth for God's people to live

Out their days for eternity;

We will be able to travel back and to

From earth to heaven in the blink of an eye,

But heaven will always be my home

For that is where my Lord and Savior

And my God lives; but I will not worry-

Earth is the footstool of God,

And He and Jesus shall walk with us

Down the beach making footprints

In the sand; but there will now

Be two sets of prints for eternity;

And though God does not have to,

Once and a while out of the blue

He shall carry us as He always has;

And it will remind us how much we love him

Because He is our Father in Heaven-

His love for us lives forever,

And we will never again know

Pain nor suffering but only peace;

And we will never again be incomplete

But will now and for eternity be whole

Part II Broken Peace: **Trials of the Chosen One**

Ba` Nee` Kou`: **The Awakening**

The light is beginning to fade

Darkness comes for me, to devour-

I am alone, solo in these last moments

As my heart beats its last;

My lungs cannot take in enough air

My breath has become short-

The silence surrounds me, emptiness;

Cold and distant are all I have become

Losing my way as I struggled till the end-

Loneliness has crept in, to take control

Of all that is left of my frail body and soul;

My words are not my own-

The voice in my head grows, whispering

The darkness is about to engulf me,

Devouring my spirit, casting away my faith,

A faith that has lost its way as I have;

With nothing by my side,

Neither angel nor demon, not Satan or Jesus,

Nor God himself; I am- I have found

The fence that never existed;

I follow the teachings of Jesus-

I live the path, but I fought the demon

Within and he won but lost his world;

The truth and the lie, one in the same-

Yet good and evil are two paths,

Given by God but only one

Is of Him and His law;

I gave in to the darkness,

And still try to follow God's commandments-

Who am I? What am I?

The demon within is all I have left-

All, even the darkness, waits for me;

I am neither in the box nor out of the box-

For I have become the box,

And the emptiness within is my future;

My demon jumps out, leaves me behind

As the darkness completes its feast;

I am no more, dead and alive-

Scorned and damned eternity,

And in the end, I realize that

All I fear is me

Infractus Pacis

With a hand reaching out,

An empty soul cries

As the day draws near;

A broken heart trembles in shame,

And the fear of blame shows its face

For life and death are the same

And neither happens for this reason;

The empty soul never sees the other

Or even the first, and the hate-

As love is lost and darkness comes,

A tired mind tries to find

Its way out of a bottomless pit;

For Heaven and Hell are never to be

A place where I shall freely see,

And the price I have paid

To win this war

Has thrown my empty dark soul

Into the outer darkness

Where even Satan fears to go;

And I have become to know

That God is far away from here,

And I realize that I am alone;

For the life I once knew

Was not mine to give up,

And the life I have now

Is only an illusion of reality;

The future is already set

As the endless cycle of chaos

Rules over all as God sits in wait

To alone set things right;

But my fate is known-

My destined life is alone;

And love- hate, peace- war,

And life- death are illusions,

All the same, all ideas

Never understood for who they are;

For winning the battle within,

Can only happen

By the loss of all- even God;

And to gain what isn't mine

Is not my course but it is my illusion

Made manifest by God's will;

And the key to it all

Is in the fear I have of myself alone

Breaking Point

The anger, the hatred

That stirs in my soul

Of myself, my life-

The very way of my being;

Lost in the thoughts of death

To myself, to others-

The madness that bellows

Within my mind;

I cannot begin to understand,

To control- I fear the worse;

I fear I may hurt someone

Close to me or myself;

I struggle to control the urge

To hit, to beat, to lose myself

In the Hell I have created-

I am not well, not who

I was before this-

This overwhelming desire of pain;

Even the slightest thing

Can trigger the burn, the yearn

To mutilate something-

I have become violent,

But only in my thoughts;

For to lash out and harm,

Is like killing any hope of

Saving what is left of my

Frail body, mind, and soul;

I dare not let anyone know

How far I have let the anger grow;

I dare not tell a soul-

For if I did, I would lose;

Yet if I do not, I will lose-

The question lingers

With no answer but God;

I have lost Him or

What He represents-

For if there is a God or not

Is not the question to ask;

All life comes from a higher source,

And life is a mere illusion

Of the human mind-

But if there is a God

And I have lost my salvation,

The Hell that waits

Is worse than the Hell I have now;

All I have left is hate and anger,

And I am scared-

For myself, for others;

My stressed life of pleasing others

Balancing work, school, family, God-

I have been absorbed by the first two,

Losing the rest;

I do not know myself anymore;

I was once a powerful and

Spiritual being, close to God-

I had become wise beyond my years,

And I had knowledge that people dream of;

Now I have lost that;

Reduced to a lifeless soul-

Tired, angered, stressed from living;

I once thought of suicide,

But my upbringing would not allow

Such a thing; I now wish

To die, and end this life-

But in a way, I wish to live

To somehow hope I will pull through;

All hope is lost; God is gone-

The Spirit, the Holy Maculate Spirit

Will never return; my only way

Into Heaven is by the grace

Of God- it too soon gone;

I have nothing to live for,

Yet, everything to loose-

My world has become a paradox;

No way in or out; no way

To win or lose- just an empty shell;

I no longer have the strength

To carry on with life

And no courage to end it;

I fear the strain of the battle

Will soon take its toll,

And I will harm those I love

Or harm myself;

Reduced to what I am now,

Alone and scared-

The darkness creeps in;

The hiding has become unbearable;

I am at war within myself-

With no end in sight,

I went into exile

Until I can become whole again-

Until I face my fears,

And give up my struggle-

To release all to the higher power,

To reach my bottomless pit's bottom

And face my inner demons;

Then and only then will I gain

A piece of my puzzle

Back from the depths of Hell-

Reclaiming my life

Or lose all to death

The Punishment

I stand in the shadows

Of my once graceful life

Where Jesus and I once walked

On the endless sands of time;

God has taken His grace

From my frail soul's beating heart,

And I walk along the path

With an empty feeling inside;

A shell is all that is left-

With a faint heart beat in my chest,

I am but a fragment of the life I once owned

A soulless mortal-

Yet- could it be?

Am I more then I appear to be?

All the weight of my sins I carry now-

If it were beef in pounds

I could end hunger on earth;

The broken promises and shattered dreams

Of turning my life around,

Haunt my walk;

Every step takes me to hell-

Every step takes me further from Jesus-

Soon there will be no more chances

No more forgive me's;

BROKEN PEACE: TRAILS OF THE CHOSEN ONE

Do I fear it,

Or am I too far gone to see?

Could this be the ultimate test?

All I see is punishment!

Ten years have gone-

Alone and without a companion;

I cannot find anyone-

Is it fate? Or is it God?

I cannot feel grace now;

I cannot feel the Holy Ghost either-

Soon even Jesus will shun me

But is that all? Can I find the light?

One thing after another-

My life falls from the sky

With no end to the torment;

The endless pain of defeat-

I am not even comforted

By words from those I love;

The war within myself

Brought by Lucifer feels lost;

I cannot see the end;

All is lost-

Will anyone, anything

Help me out of the pit I have dug-

So much lost time

With my family, Jesus, and God;

THE CHOSEN ONE

I do not dare let a soul know

How far I have gone-

But if I do not seek and find help,

I will be lost forever;

Truly this is punishment!

The whisper in my head

Tells me to press on,

Fight with all my strength

Until I cannot fight no more-

But I am without strength;

I cannot press on,

I am weak-

Each step hurts more and more,

Like walking on broken glass-

Like swimming through hot lava;

I can no longer carry the burden

Of my tribulations;

God does not give more than

A man can carry,

Surely the extra trials-

The extra tribulations

Are punishment for my unwillingness;

I am stagnate- stuck;

I am like a rock stuck in the side of a stream-

The water withers away my layers

Bit by bit until I am no more,

BROKEN PEACE: TRAILS OF THE CHOSEN ONE

I fold my hands-

Cash in my last chips-

Hoping I will not walk away

Without a bit of hope;

So I push further

Feeling pain with every step-

Hoping I will regain a bit of grace

To carry me home

The Voice

Silent, cold, the slumber;

Night- the stars,

Out of body, out of mind,

The soul- asleep and feared;

Awakened by light-

The Shadow- the Sun-

The wet lucid dream of my life-

Do I hear? Will I hear?

The whisper, the wind's song;

Have I seen? Or have I dreamed?

The silent, the cold inferno of fire-

Warmth of my heart-

The desire, the anguish,

Perplexity's calling,

Convoluted, distant-

I am alone- I am forgotten-

I am dead

The Calling

My time has come-

The end comes soon;

Time for the choice, my choice-

My darkness has consumed me;

The enemy, Lucifer, has used me

Even as I fight him;

He convolutes my failing faith-

I have lost my strength,

I have lost my way-

Can I come out of the darkness?

Can I find the light?

I can no longer see my light,

No longer do I hear Jesus' voice calling;

The spirit has left me,

And God calls grace away;

The battle has overwhelmed me-

My body and soul cries out in pain,

My trials torment them,

And my tribulations have become more then I can bear;

Will I ever see myself out of the darkness?

Will I again see my light?

I can no longer feel the calling-

I am lost in my own hell;

There is no more strength,

And my faith is lost;

Is there a way out of my hell?

Is there anything left to strengthen me?

I can still hear the soul's cry

That I never saved-

I can still feel their pain

As they are tormented by my enemy;

But how can I save them now?

How can I save myself?

Do I dare push forward?

Can I push forward?

My soul is battered and torn,

My body is frail and weak-

I have destroyed God's temple with my sin,

I have allowed myself to be tainted

By the one I fight, Lucifer;

He is winning the battles

As the war rages on-

There is no rock to rest my weary soul upon,

No vine to pull myself out of the quicksand;

I am alone in my struggle-

All I have left is my failing faith;

But is that enough to pull me out of my hell?

Can I find something inside to strengthen me?

Is there enough light in me?

I look deep inside- searching for

The last mountaintop I was on;

I focus on that moment,

A time where I could hear Jesus calling,

A time where the spirit flowed through me,

A time where God's grace carried me;

My light begins to strengthen-

I push forward with only my frail faith

Until I find a rock to rest my soul upon,

Until I can again see the light,

Until I am out of my hell;

The way is hard- every step brings pain;

My soul imagines a time

When there are no more valleys,

When I can hear Jesus' voice,

When the spirit dwells in me,

And God's grace carries me

As my calling is fulfilled;

The souls I never saved to reach heaven-

My body and soul gains strength

Because they know a day will come

Where my enemy, Lucifer,

Gets thrown into Hell-

And I will stand before the gates to heaven,

And walk into paradise

Where my God waits for me

Psalm 152: **Psalm of the Chosen One for the Warriors**

Glory to God in the highest,

For you raised me up from the ashes,

You brought me out of the pits of hell,

You gave me my strength against my enemies,

Praises to Lord God all mighty;

Hear me warriors of the Lord!

Sing praises unto Your God

For He is worthy of our praise;

He has brought us victory,

He has guided us through our battles,

He gives us strength,

Give thanks to the Lord;

I say unto you my brethren,

Keep your faith in our God

For He shall deliver us

From our enemies;

Do not lose sight of the promise land,

Do not forsake His teachings;

We shall pray and fast,

We shall ask His forgiveness

Before each battle;

Praises to God almighty;

We sing songs of Your love,

We worship You

With all our heart and voice;

Hear us O' Lord,

Send Your angels to us,

Give us victory over our enemies,

Guide us so we do not lose

Sight of our calling;

Hear me O' warriors of the Lord our God,

Clear your thoughts of vengeance and anger

For they will pull you to the darkness

Where your enemies dwell;

Be weary and cautious of the shadows

For that is where they hide,

Be slow to act,

Do not rush into battle

For hastening will weaken us;

Behold my Lord our God,

Your warriors stand ready to fight;

Hear them O' Lord

For they sing praises unto Your name;

Look inside me O' Lord my God,

Help me not to be tempted,

Give me knowledge and wisdom

To lead Your army in battle;

Let us all rejoice in You O' Lord

For You are worthy of our praises;

You shall lead us to victory,

You shall lead us to paradise;

We honor You with our song,

We shall give thanks to You O' Lord,

Be with us in our hour of need;

Amen

www.ingramcontent.com/pod-product-compliance
Lightning Source LLC
Chambersburg PA
CBHW031328040426
42443CB00005B/258